ODE TO
MY NODE:

A POETRY BOOK
ABOUT CANCER

BY S. J. GOODERHAM

*This one's for you.
You are not alone in this
We're in this together*

SG
1994
S. GOODERHAM
TOUJOURS EN AVANT

For Molly Norton;

Close Friends
never leave.

They still exist
in the stars

Words Hold Power (And So Do We)

CONTENTS

CONTENTS

THIS IS IT

Everything moved in slow motion.
Sounds became muffled.
The room was a white blur under florescent lights.
The air sucked out. Time stood still momentarily.
The dark slit of the door started to expand
emerged a man in a white coat walking in
with papers in hand.
All I saw peeking out among the stack
was a pamphlet
with one bold word on the cover.
Before the Doctor could even utter a word
or had the chance to sit down
I already knew,

This is it.

YOU WAKE UP

Monday to Friday
9:00 am to 5:00 pm.

Oh the places you'll go.
Drive around a city
with too many roads
on a highway feeling low.

This can't be it.

Love songs for robots
Play on the radio.
You whistle along
like a big bird in a small cage
that sings the best tune.
Humming Patrick Watson's
The Great Escape.

Stuck in traffic of stop and go.

Remind yourself to dream.
To have a goal
To get the job to get the car
to meet a man to drive home.
Together
To get a house to make it a home
to have the kids to have a life.

Hi Name,
Hope all is well.
It's Sarah calling from The Business Company ™
I was wondering if you had any listings
you wanted to advertise in
The Spring Edition of The Magazine ™

The script.
I said 150 - 200 times a day.

9:00am to 5:00pm
But it was never just those hours…
Monday to Friday
But it never was just those days…
For lunch, I have a doctor's appointment
So I leave work early.

I left my cubicle.
A small win over the dull monotony of the mundane
even if it was just for a check-up.
It was still better than the droning endless
cold calling that filled most of my days.

R/LIMINALSPACE

You know the feeling, that uneasy vibe of
'not knowing what's up but something is definitely up.'

It's eerie and you can't place it.

This vacant familiar feeling…

These places
that feel strangely familiar
although you've never been before

Online images of

Bowling alleys
Old arcades
An abandoned mall
A park or parking lot at night
The office past office hours
A rainy traffic jam
with the wiper sounds
others in cars splashing past.
Stuck at a red light,
watching the rain drops
race down the windows
hoping your drop wins

If these sound familiar
Consult your doctor
you may have encountered
a liminal space

These memories belong to everybody and nobody

Of course, the bottom of the page is a potential place
but the most prominent one of all?

THE WAITING ROOM

I'm sitting in the waiting room
these places are all the same.

Stale magazines, old furniture and "art"
that isn't really art.

She'll call my name
I'll walk away from the others waiting.
Walk into the office.
The standard questions will go like this

"How is your mood?"
"Are you exercising?"
"Has anything changed?"

I'll get a prescription
take the pills
till I can wean off them.
Tell no one and move on.
in-and-out.
Back to the 9 to 5.
Save up.
Have a life
I want to live.

I look around the waiting room.
Drugged out zombies
I'm not like them.

I'm not like the others.
I'll get out of this.
I'll get better.

I think back to my hospital stay.

I remember the coffee
a powder packet, decaf of course.
Wooden stir-sticks and white styrofoam cups.

Hospitals and waiting rooms
have a special kind of energy.

A liminal space of the 'what was' and 'what's next.'
Betwixt and between
the familiar and the completely unknown.
A place of transition,
a season of waiting, and uncertainty.

Soon, alone our old-world is left behind.

These thresholds of waiting…

Reality isn't quite what it seems.
Normality isn't quite what it used to be
(at least for me).

Not quite what it was.
Not knowing what is next.

Living life in between chapters

caught in the subtext.

Soon, she'll call my name.

These places by design
all look the same
because if you're waiting here

Your reality may shatter
The last worry won't even matter
Because before you knew it

everything has already changed.

SILENCE

Before there was nothing,
there was silence.

Silence has no mass but can fill a room.
It can feel like a conversation's doom.
It is an expression, one that cannot be heard.
Silence cannot be spoken although it is a word.

Silence is a presence of great nothingness.
Silence can be something
and yet cease to exist.

Silence is the sound of rest
the only sound that can sound best.

Others claim it causes great pain.
Silence is not the sound to blame.
For silence is what silence is
Something that is nothing,
nothing that exists.

HOW TO RIDE A BIKE

Before I learned how to ride a bike
I was taught what is and isn't lady-like.
A light frame that must steer down the right road
with generations of women passing on these codes.

"Don't speak unless spoken to."
"Must say please and thank you."

The essence of a man can span
while woman must woo-man?
Why is it his-story and not her story?
Because it isn't filled with pride and glory

It's about
a rock and a hard place.
A woman and a small space.

Silence is a woman.
She, who is not to be heard
even when she speaks a word.
It's accepted as nothingness.
Seeing her for lesser than less.

Silence is a little girl.
Put on low-fat diets. Sugar free.
Calculated calories
before learning chemistry.
Ashamed when she shouldn't be.

Advertised as surface pretty.
I think that's pretty petty.
"Zero" given as a size
to be seen as nothing in disguise
for keeping women
small and marginalized.

It's lunchtime and I'm starving.
I want to order CHANGE
with fries on the side.

I want
to tailor the size
of my mind
not to think
of the thickness
of my thighs.

I eat
flavors of hard labour
that it took to put
health to my mouth.

I want
to feel my surroundings
not have my surroundings
surround me.

I flip through the pages
of many pretty girls
with hollow faces.

Ads categorize us by a size.
And yet Photoshop
the pain out of our eyes.

Here's an appetizer…
Let's starve these advertisers.

I pick up a different magazine
in the waiting room.

The headline titled
HEALTH.

THIS IS IT

In walked Doctor Simone.
He was a handsome man,
middle aged, married of course,
with warmth to him that can be rare.
He had proper bedside manner.
He printed out my scan
sat with my Mom and I,
making sure we could see what he did
the black and white
grey blob image
was my chest.
He said,

"This is your heart
these are your lungs
here is your thyroid."

Using a pen to circle
"This is a tumor and also here too."
the lump in my throat was not just a feeling
it was real and it metastasized.
You have a tumor in your neck just under your thyroid
and one in your chest right behind the sternum.
My Mom and I looked at each other
wanting permission from the other to cry
but neither of us wanted to be the first to break
so we didn't.
We keep our trauma casual.

My Dad walked in very causally
talking about how hard
it is to find parking in Toronto
how expensive it is
to park here.

Dr. Simone shook my Dad's hand
I reheard the news for the second time.
They talked about some hockey player that had the same
diagnosis that I was just given. How very Canadian and
casual, like I said we keep our trauma casual.
Just shooting the shit: "Oh cancer, eh?"

It's a bit of a blur now but all I remember is
hearing him say,

"The lab technicians and I were so happy when we found
out.
We were almost jumping up and down."

My face scrunched up, I didn't know anything about can-
cer except that the movies portray it as the worst fucking
thing, that it's like one sneeze away from death.
I picture all these doctors in white coats jumping for joy
then huddled in a big circle swaying and singing,
"Kumbaya my Lord, kumbaya…"
As they find out my cancer diagnosis.
I was perplexed to say the least.
I just got hit with a type of cancer and this man is
celebrating?
He handed me a pamphlet with one bold word
on the cover,

Lymphoma.
He continued and corrected himself by saying,

"We were relieved it was lymphoma because we all
thought it was fatal."

Later that week,
I'd had another appointment scheduled with my family
doctor,
who didn't know I had already heard the news,
so I would hear this uttered for the third time.
When my family doctor had said it, she was very nervous.
Her voice was shaky and serious.
When I looked her in the eyes and gave a delicate smile I
said,

"I already know."
Her whole body sighed in relief that she didn't have to be
the one to break it to me.
The tension was gone.

"Oh you already know?"

This is my heart.
These are my lungs.
Here is my tumor
there is another one here too.
The first time my heart broke
was when a boy in my class
had died in a car accident.
We liked each other.
It was in December.
He visited me in my dreams the night he died.
It was winter but in my dream it was summer.
He was glowing from what I thought was the sun
As we waited in our lines to load the school bus,
He said while waving and smiling,
"Bye Sarah."
I thought, I'll see you tomorrow Daniel.
We were 10 years old.

His funeral was the first ever one I had been to.
It was at a synagogue.
The Rabbi was saying sentiments while his Mother dis-
played the truest form of grief
I had ever witnessed to this day. Openly howling and asking
the Rabbi
"Why?!"
She had just lost two sons.
First, Daniel's older brother who was beaten to death
over a pack of cigarettes by senseless teenagers.
Now Daniel.
She had one son left, a baby.
Daniel had asked for another sibling after his older broth-
er's passing,
someone he could play with.
That was the first time I felt a lump in my throat, tightness
from sadness.
His Father had survived the car crash but Daniel didn't.
Those of us from class who attended went up to speak.
I don't remember what I said but I remember he always
wanted to be a writer so
Hey Daniel, this one's for you:

The first time my lungs hurt was when we were running
outside in the playground playing tag.

I never knew bad things could happen
to people you know.
Tag, you were it.

As a kid, I always thought bad things
only happen to other people.
People you never knew.
Those people.
The others.

THE OTHERS

Urban legends.
Stories that happened to
a friend of a friend of mine.

The Others.
Those people where
the unimaginable,
the unthinkable
things that only ever
happens to them
happened to them.

You see them on the news.
Read about them in the papers.
By-passers. Strangers.
The foggy backdrop people of life
that you've never seen.
Blurry faces.
People you never knew.

They are the ones with those stories you hear.
Strange things only happen to them.

The Others.
The outskirts.
The fringes and the fray
pulling on threads that make up the fabric of your reality.

You only ever hear about them from
a friend of a friend of mine.
Who's uncle's boss's cousin's neighbour's best friend's
mother
tells a story…

The unimaginable.
The unthinkable things
that only happens to them.

Not me.
Nothing ever happens to me.
But can it?

Things only happen to other people.
Not you.
Nothing ever happens to you.

But can it?

Urban legends.
Stories that happened to a
friend of a friend of mine.

This time it's you.

Your story is the unimaginable,
the unthinkable thing
that happens.

Hello, I am the friend of a friend that it happened to.
I hope my story doesn't end like your friend of a friend's
sister's neighbour's grandma's dog that it happened to.

You are part of The Others now.
The others start to reveal themselves.
They are still vague stories but this time it's…

Those people. Died of cancer.
You already knew that was coming.
Look how lucky you are.
You could be dead
is the moral of each story
If I were dead
I wouldn't have to have this conversation.
You are part of The Others now.

The unimaginable.
The unthinkable things
that only happens to them
happened to you.

You shock those
that still have invincibility bubbles.
They walk past you.
The foggy backdrop people of life.
By-passers. Strangers. The people
that haven't had their bubble burst, just quite yet.

THE OTHERS:

My Boss's Neighbour's
Sister's Cousin's Friend's Mother's Dog
Had lymphoma...he died.

"PLEASE HAVE A SEAT."

"Dr. Normal will see you shortly."

"Dr. Normal?" I thought I heard at first.

I continued over to the receptionist who gestured me to
the waiting area.

I was very skeptical, if not cynical about attending a ses-
sion.

I didn't like the idea of someone thinking that because
they read a textbook and passed a few tests that
they could ever know the deep inner workings of the
human condition,
let alone psychoanalyze me.

I was lucky enough to be treated at one of the top cancer
hospitals in the world,
which to me sounds like they get a lot of funding.
As a result, I was given some free therapy sessions.
Otherwise there is no way I could ever afford it.

Dr. Norma walked in.
She was fairly tall
with brown hair that fell to her shoulders.
She wore glasses and was younger than I expected,
early 40s.
She appeared stuffy but slouched her hip to give off a

casual "I'm cool" vibe,
like she was fighting her whole life not to be the stereo-
typical
classic look of a therapist or even librarian.
I got up from the waiting room chair and she guided me
down the hallway to the room.

She opened the door and said,

"Pick a seat."

I looked around the room.

Chair 1: A standard looking office chair

Chair 2: a wooden rocking chair

Chair 3: The therapist's chair

Chair 4: A beige armchair

And a couch.

As if to say

"Which one are you?"

"Pick a seat"

Dr. Norma gestured.
I picked the rocking chair
She, of course, picked the Therapist's chair.
Sat down and began to settle herself in while organizing
her papers.

I almost picked her chair, just to humour myself
say something like,
"And how are you feeling? hOw iS yOuR MOoD?"

"So how are you handling things?
She asked.
"How did your friends and family react to the news?
How did you tell people?"

I take out my phone to read her the Facebook post I
wrote to break the news.

On April 17th 2017, it went like this:
To be honest, I've been putting this off for quite some
time. Especially because I know if I have to explain this
fully it'd be one of those lengthy ass paragraphs you scroll
past then scroll back up and attempt to skim to find out
if this is a rant on some hot new political topic or some
over share of personal details. It can really only be one of
the two. This post is a personal one, mainly because I'm
tired of one-on-one explaining to everyone that,

I have cancer, bam there I said it.

February 24th of this year, I was diagnosed with Hodgkin's Lymphoma cancer.
If you've made it this far in reading I'm very impressed
and consider yourself cool. If you're curious on how I
found out, there was this hard painless lump on the base
of my neck. No it's not an Adam's apple but an enlarged
lymph node or tumor so I thought I should probably get
it checked out.
Thus, began the medical escapade of …

Ultra sounds
Countless blood work tests
3 CT scans
3 biopsies
1 PET scan
and a partridge in a pear tree

The PET scan showed that the cancer is in my throat and chest and possibly in my groin so I could be anywhere from a stage 1 to a stage 3. I start chemotherapy this Wednesday April 19th before I even know what stage I am or how many months of chemo I'll have to do. Will I need surgery or radiation?
If life were perfect I would have already known my staging before getting thrown into chemotherapy treatment and if life was really perfect I wouldn't have this shitty diagnosis but I guess,

"We cannot direct the wind but we can adjust the sails…"

So if you've made it this far in the book, consider yourself cool.
Thank you
now keep reading.
So chemo is 4 - 8 hours long and what would be cool is if people post songs I could check out while I'm sitting in a chair getting pumped full of poison. There is no judgement, I like all music even if it's sad and I can tolerate country music, kind of, but yeah I just want to expand my music taste because it's getting old. You can comment below or inbox me. It'd be greatly appreciated.
I also want to thank everyone for the wonderful support and positive energy even the most simple gestures have gone a long way and are cherished. I still find myself

laughing about the inevitable outcomes that life brings. So
Thank You.

Hundreds of comments with links to songs, personalized
playlists, an influx of personal messages, phone calls that
lead to weeping voicemails. Love, prayers, and support
were received.
I chose to ask for songs because…there is no right thing
to say.

There are no right words.
I wanted people to reach out even if they didn't know
what to say…

Just send a song

We remember the feeling rather than the right words said.
And I wanted the feeling with the volume turned all the
way up.

Life is like a musical, we end with a final song played at
our funeral but right now I'm just trying to find the right
soundtrack to my life because my life's been on pause…

THE GOOD CANCER ™

Congratulations! I think?
I heard the good news
You've got
The Good Cancer ™

That's like the good one to get, right?
It's less…
Well you probably won't…

Oh…
You have to freeze your eggs
You still have to do chemotherapy
Will you loose your hair?
Oh…
Well you can get cool wigs, that's good.

The Good Cancer isn't that good
I'm sure if you could
No one would
Pick a cancer
because cancer ain't that good

The Gooderham from the hood
got The Good Cancer **™**
Do you know her? S.Goodz

I heard an oxymoron say:

"Isn't that The Good Cancer **™**?"

Cancer can't be that good
Especially if it hit you in childhood
Or a friend from your neighborhood
Or a homie in the hood

The Cancer ain't that good.
The sentiment is a bit misunderstood
It affects your livelihood
The Good Cancer **™** is a falsehood

Thank you for your opinion
That I didn't ask for
Thanks for the story
The tips for sickness
You've never had before
You're trying to help
That's very nice
You've got all the tricks
But I didn't ask to be fixed
by your unsolicited advice.

I just wanted to be heard
but as soon as they heard
the cancer word
it's something else to try
Thank you, it's worth a try
If it doesn't work

Please don't cry

WHAT IS A LYMPHOMIE?

Lymphomie: a lymphomie is a friend with cancer. Typically an online friend, one diagnosed with a form of lymphoma. Abbreviated word for "lymphoma-homie."

Synonymous with: 'cancer patient' or 'cancer survivor.'

"LOST THEIR BATTLE"

Everything felt like a *paradox*
so contradictive and stupid.
My life turned into someone else watching a movie play
out.

This paradox:
With eyes wide shut, *act natural*
Like it's your *only choice*.
Trying to *force* a *genuine* conversation with people.
Being *bitterly positive*.
"Stay positive," they say.
 "Stay strong," yet bedridden
Good cancer.

Lately, I've been feeling like an insomniac singing lullabies
trying to help those sleep.

The imposter syndrome is real.

I'm not some soldier.
I don't like the terminology that comes with cancer.

This isn't a war, it's an illness.

I don't want a fight song,
I want proper medicine and rest.

We need a cure not another battle scene.

We are fighting to stay alive but also merely experiencing it too.
I didn't do anything different than those that did die, so telling me I'm a strong fighter makes me feel like a fraud. All I could do was keep the vibes right.

In war, there has to be a winner and a loser.

Cancer to me, doesn't feel honorable or heroic.
It just feels random and chaotic.
It's a bunch of shit that happens to you.
Not some game I was an active participant in.

'The Battle language' I believe was incentivized in the 1950's as a way to promote funding for cancer research after the second war but now it just feels outdated and harsh. If I did die from cancer and someone said,

"She lost her battle to cancer."
Y'all are getting haunted.

Cancer feels more nuclear,
not just because of the radiation
but because…

In the cancer community, there are no winners just survivors.

Grief Tourist: a broad term applied to the practice of people who "pay respect" or "come out of the woodwork" **superficially**. They swoop in providing no true support or help. They are those who were never close to the sick and/or deceased. Typically, they are the people you don't know very well and they wouldn't have cared about you otherwise. They just like the attention.

Reminder: There is a difference between care vs. curiosity. Be kind no matter the reason and know your boundaries with people. Of course, there are one's who are genuine that do send love, prayers, a friendly hello even and are truly thinking of you. Let's face it, it's nice to be thought of. Life isn't a one-way-street of only caring about you either.

Confession: It can be exhausting making people feel seen for reaching out to you. Handling their feelings while still processing your own. At the time, I had no boundaries with people and felt drained if I wasn't controlling the narrative of this cancer.

Remember: People are in your life for a season, a reason, or a lifetime.

The rest will sort itself out.

LIFE + LEMONS:
When Life Gives You Lemons…

WHEN LIFE GIVES YOU LEMONS...

Start a YouTube Channel.
About how you got cancer and blame it on chainmail. Darn, you never sent that message to ten people by 11:59PM that one time. Great, now you have cancer.

When life gives you lemons, take those lemons and start throwing them at the shitty people who assumed your diet and negativity caused this. Shove one right up the ass of those who tell you to "stay positive." Then ask them to stay positive with a lemon up their ass the ENTIRE time too. Whip a juicy bad boy at those who tell you their friend's cousin's boss's neighbour cured their cancer with moondust and rare jungle-fruit found in the outskirts of Africa or Australia or whatever. Squeeze the lemon juice into the cuts of those who tell you how pretty your hair *was*. Chuck one at the heads of those asking when you're going back to work.

And finally, keep a lemon…to freeze because I heard that frozen lemons are all the rage and the new trend of curing your cancer. But seriously, keep one for you. Do whatever you wish to do with it. My suggestion is slice it up, place it on top of tequila shots and pass some around to those you love and those who love you.
Cheers!

You'll need it because cancer is…
One hell of a ride or a "J O U R N E Y."

Sending all the good vibes, thoughts and prayers your way!
You've got this! [Glitter emoji + flexing muscle arm emoji]

Love,
Sgoodz

THE INTERNET, OPEN 24/7

I'd talk to cancer patients and survivors
All from different time zones
It allowed me to time travel
move forward and back in time
At this point
all my social interactions were online
Too weak and sick to see anyone in person

I lived online
while living on the line
a type rope balance of life or death
kill or be killed.
Balancing killing the cancer
And not to be killed from the cancer

I'd lie awake in Toronto
the time 12:33am
Click out of my reality
Talk to someone
In France,
the time 6:33 am
someone starting their morning
With the fresh smells of breakfast
Buttery, doughy, flaky croissants, warmed up
Paired with a French pressed coffee
Poured into a porcelain white cup
Glide to another part of The Internet galaxy
Take a glimpse into Greece at 7:33 am

Have an Australian afternoon at 4: 33 pm
All in the same minute
We see so many different lives
We see so many different stories
all in the same minute
all the time online
I could find someone to talk to anytime
All the time and so I did
I was an insomniac from all the drugs anyway so
The Internet and this illness combined
Opened a new portal
A new place
The Somewhere Else
An escape
Momentarily
Mentally
though the physical remained the same
I fell down internet rabbit holes
kept my brain entertained
a great distraction away from pain
Click in. Click out.
Again and again
A minute online is not the same
Time is diversely relative
in The Internet Age
Click in. Click out.
Again and again.

OUR LITTLE DANCE

You log in
I log out

Check in
Click out

Click in
Look in

I log in
You log out.

We do this dance to pretend
we aren't so desperate
for real life attention
in hopes that we can click each other
into our next life chapter
I'll follow if you do.

I'll like if you like me too.

I'll leave you little comments
that will be forgotten
as time and technology progresses.

You see me

stuck on the screen.

I'll leave you a comment
or be more direct
with my direct messages

like

like

heart shape

I type to you
like I love you

like
we like each other
like each word
sent
is an engraving in stone
on a grey tablet
like
our ancient ancestors
used to draw on walls
and carve hearts in trees

this connection

we like

we type

like

You're my typing type

like I like like you type
the type I like to type to

trying to come up with jokes to send you
sending memes you haven't seen
I know for a fact as I'm

stuck on a screen.

[Storage full]

Clear some memories
maybe I'll have room for you
but I'm still alone in my room.

YOU LOG IN

High above the ivory tower
There is a cloud without rain
Yet still collects.

Data.

Found.

iCloud my mind with made up stories.
iPhone, iHome, I leave.

In a world of online fantasy,
Believe in yourself.

Don't get sucked into
Signaling…
Virtual virtues ready to cancel one another.
All from an ivory cell tower
Sending…
From a gilded phone
Typing...
The black mirror reflects our worst nightmares.

How social are the fairytale lives
We tell ourselves and post online.

How social is the algorithm?
Starving for attention in feedback loops.

Echo chambers are the new dungeons.
We are flooded.
Give me a like and I'll love you later.

All the trolls from under the bridge went online,
they're such haters.

People ought to power down to power up?
Stop listening to the rich tech executives
who are morally bankrupt.
Soulless endless scrolling...

Click in. click out.

THE DIGITAL WORLD.

Another app.
Same difference.
By design.

Free to spend all my time.
Data harvest all that's mine.

If it is free, you are the product.

Narcissistic by nurture.
Convenience over privacy?
Can they see me?
Just to be safe
I cover my webcam.
My social life vacancy.

Snapchat's icon is a ghost.
As if to say we've become transparent
but through filters simultaneously loose ourselves.
Our uniqueness masked.
Maybe I'm just using it wrong?

I log out.

AN EMAIL TO
MY THERAPIST:

Wed Nov 22 2018 at 1:35 am

Hi Norma,

I'm not feeling the best and I thought I would see if venting would help.
So it seems, I'm pretty depressed. I find myself lying in bed, staring at nothing with the curtains drawn in a cluttered dim room. When I'm not doing that I'm eating or sleeping or trying to watch something to distract myself from the idea that each day just passes by.

I'm in this limbo stage of not really taking control of living my life in anticipation of something shitty happening again, whether that's relapse or … who knows.

I know that many cancer survivors feel this guilt paradox and conundrum of the jinx syndrome; it's hard to move forward or change anything because the cancer might return. I can't let myself get too happy because I'm worried life will come back and bite me in the ass for being too optimistic. So I'm not living, I'm just watching days pass with little interaction. The kicker is I wish I had some form of intimacy, a boyfriend to lie with and turn over to his side of the bed and find comfort. Or have a friend I can call in the middle of the night and cry with. I have so much uncertainty in my life. I'm sure,

"It's all temporary."
I tell myself and hate shedding the slightest light on how
truly sad I am but I don't know what else to do. I get nervous letting on how sad I can be. Ultimately, I think I just
need to go out and find new interactions I guess because:

We don't see people anymore
We see screens of them

I'm just a girl in a computer to most
Drag, drop, click out and close
only seeing me when I post
one of many;
I am an Internet ghost.

Nothing in bed but the blue-ish white glow of my laptop
I want to see someone with the brightness turned down
I want to touch, not tap my screen, to show I'm around.

There's a little random poem in the middle of a teary-in-
duced ramble.
Anyways, I'm seeing a doctor tomorrow because I lost my
prescriptions to Ativan, Zopiclone, and Valium so hope-
fully he will prescribe one if not all again and maybe I can
chill out for a bit. I don't expect you to have all the answers
and I get that you're very busy so just being heard is nice
so thank you.

All the best,
Sarah

Automatic reply:

I am currently out of the office. I will respond to your message as soon as possible upon my return on Nov. 26. 2018.

If you are a pediatric after care patient and need more immediate assistance and you can call the psychosocial oncology reception desk at xxx-xxx-xxxx. Alternatively, you can call the reception desk at xxx-xxx-xxxx.

If this is an emergency please call 911 or proceed to your local emergency room.

Thank you,
Dr. Norma

***

"I thought I was gonna win the lottery
today ... but I didn't, so that kind of
ruined my plans ..."

WHAT IT FEELS LIKE

If you've ever wanted to know what chemotherapy feels like
It's having your period
while getting hit by a car
that's getting hit by a bus
on your way home from getting fired after breaking up,
and puking, crying, and dying a little inside
All at the same time…

It's the unimaginable, unthinkable suffering and pain.

Oddly enough, you get used to it.

Chemotherapy is a combination of different cocktails of drugs.
I always thought chemo-treatment was a "one size fits all" but that isn't the case.
There are categories such as, Immunotherapy, hormonal therapy, targeted therapy, and cytotoxic chemotherapy. Other terms that I'm aware of are drug combinations of chemotherapy like:
- ABVD
- R-CHOP
- STEM cell transplant

Honourable mentions that are commonly used to kill cancer cells while trying not to kill the patient simultaneously are:
- Adriamycin (red kool-aid bag)

- Prednisone (devil's tic-tac)
- Doxorubicin (a classic)
- Methotrexate (I'd be telling everyone I'm on meth)

And many other names that sound like transformer names…
Talk to your doctor, I don't know sh*t.

LIVING & DYING
AT THE SAME TIME

I'm sitting in the waiting room
with other cancer patients.
We're all gray in complexion
With little or no hair left on our cold aching bodies.
Most are old.
I try not to make eye contact because
I've gotten really good at knowing
who will make it and who won't.
And I don't want to know or let on.
I've seen too many profiles with eyes that tell
Talk to my soul and stop in for a quick chat only to go
Forever offline.
So my eyes shift around not staying too long on much.
I want little memory of this place
Little to no stimulation the better
The less I'll remember.
I stare at a basket of yarn; someone must have left this for
us.
Something to do while we wait.
We wait long hours in the waiting room.
You hear beeps and the hospital intercom come on
a code tied to a colour to tell you what type of emergency
this is.
We are numbers taking letters.
Stage 2, taking ABVD.
The intercom comes on with an automated voice

CODE WHITE: MEDICAL EMERGENCY (PEDIATRIC)

I hold my breath and pray.
A friend let me borrow an old iPod
Nostalgic songs envelop a force field
Away from this place
I press play
Let my mind play.

IT'S THE EARLY 2000S

Mid summer vacation as a preteen
Your parents went to bed
You stay up late to watch TV shows
The Simpsons at 10:30pm
That 70's Show - 11:00pm
Futurama - 11:30pm
South Park - 12:00am
That was the line up.
Flopped on the couch
snacking on salsa and nachos
These were the days of simplicity.

The living room
dimly lit by a lamp
the bright flickering glow of the TV
would fill the rest of the room.
The black plastic remote
with little rubber buttons
would be close by incase
a commercial was too loud.
The volume lowered
Do not disturb those sleeping
just loud enough
to hear the crappy
late night commercials
Like "Call Quest"
A sad service for lonely men
Far from any 'exciting quest'

I would think more of a
'call for help.'
Then a commercial for a fast food burger would play.
TV burgers always looked so tasty, especially at night.
I'd crunch down on another salty corn chip
to curve my craving for late night fast food
And the next show would start:

TV14
This program may contain one or more of the following:
suggestive dialogue (D), strong coarse language (L),
sexual situations (S), or violence (V).
Viewer discretion is advised.
I would smirk
feeling mature and immature
all at the same time.
My summer vibe.
I miss my old phone
the clunky chunky phone back
when phones were dumb
and people were smart.

If you had a question
you had to ask Jeeves.

Google it.
You couldn't
it wasn't a thing yet.

Growing up as a child in the midst of
the world's technological boom was wild.

I was never one for the social use of technology.

I had a light pink Tamagotchi I gave away.
All my Neopets starved.
I killed off all my Sims after I made them wohoo.
Although, I still have my blue Game Boy Advance SP
I only had three games:
Sweet 16 Mary Kate and Ashley Learn to Drive, yes that was a game.
American Idol and Fairy Odd Parents.
I keep these games around incase of power outs.
If you didn't understand any of what I had just said,
chances are you didn't grow up in the early 2000s or you're Amish.
All those gadgets and games are now considered outdated or obsolete.

I had a Piczo.com account
where you could make your own website.
Founded in 2003, which honestly felt like a fever dream
that so few remember.
A social networking and blogging website
for teens and pre-teens like myself.
Before MySpace and Facebook ever existed.
I spent most of my days customizing my own website
somehow taught myself basic HTML code so I could embed videos, songs, and little quizzes. I even had an extension to these avatars that became known as "Dollz," basically digital paper dolls you could dress and customize.
I was obsessed with them.
I spent hours customizing digital outfits, choosing the right hairstyle and colour.
I even had a chat log on my page where my friends could sign in and leave a comment like,
"Have a good summer!"
"So-and-so was here" type of vibe.

It was a digital yearbook and a place to hangout after school.
The theme colours were pink, blue, and yellow but mostly turquoise.
My little Digital World.
"Bluestar4ever.piczo.com"
I have no idea what happened to it.
I had no interest in joining Facebook when it first launched. It was the end of grade 7 when my best friend created my Facebook account on the last day of school. Schools were out and we were at her house sitting in front of the computer when she convinced me.

"How else are you going to keep in touch with everyone during the summer?"

"In-touch." It's funny it feels like that's all we touch now. Always keep in touch even while we are so out of touch. Disconnected yet always connected to our pocket sized digital worlds.

How did we fit humanity into such a small device?
Or did we?

We grew up right in the midst of the technological boom of Web. 2.
It's all really fascinating to step outside of it all and just look at it...

We forget that Internet Culture hasn't been around that long.
In fact, whatever happens we are the first in history to have experienced it.
Whether we used it right or wrong...

We are the first.
We are the pioneers of the World Wide Web.
It feels like some weird form of the last settlers
cultivating and forming communities.

The last Wild Wild West, www.Worldwide.com
As I'm writing this there is talk of "buying land" online in
meta-verses.

So in a way, we are all Internet Explorers.

Imagine The Internet as a Galaxy
We as stars almost colliding
These platforms are like planets.

Amazed by the limitless power
We wield on different platforms
We jump from one portal to another
Entirely different worlds
Entirely different versions of ourselves
We meet in this place.

Amazed we meet in this space.

A friend is a gift we give ourselves.

We walk alongside each other on connected paths.

Add friend. Friend request. Add friend. Friend request.

An Internet Friend is a fairly new type of gift.

My first friend was Tom from MySpace…kidding.

Having an online friend is similar in feeling to being a child with an imaginary friend – you spend countless hours talking, sharing inside jokes, and stories together.

A tucked away bond that feels very personal and yet we know it isn't.
A friendship that exists but very few see it.

Late at night, when I couldn't sleep I'd play 'what if's' with myself.

What if
imaginary friends of children
are angels watching over them?

What if
online friends
are souls that needed to connect
despite physical distance?

We live in quiet corners
Yearning
On separate screens
Cold, silver, artificial togetherness
Isolated by design
A product of our times
We want a true connection

When you're fighting illness
Hooked up to machines
Spending most of your days online
Living a half life
Time really didn't matter
quite the same way ever again
Time and space start to blur.

A little red notification appears
So I tap it.

Lymfomo – abbreviated term for "Lymphoma-fomo" that is the "fear of missing out" due to having lymphoma.

Example: All your friends are out partying and you're home bald in bed "missing out."

I remember there was a particular Friday
in the chemo chair
that was harder than most days.
I had just gotten to the point of my habitual vomiting
after the nasty red kool-aid bag had been injected into me.
I would feel the sensation of death slowly chill my veins,
muscle tissues and my bones would ache to the core.

You get cold.
Really cold.

A wave of nausea would kick in.
I would get up from the chair calmly not to alarm my Mom
or the nurses.

I would wheel my IV pole down the hallway with a coy step
to my walk, past the others sometimes smiling, winking,
flashing finger guns – just kidding.
I'd quietly and calmly open the special bathroom; only cancer patients were allowed to use it.
Segregated due to the toxic drugs

I'd see social media posts of people out drinking; having
fun, while the sight of my bright red urine would make me
vomit on cue.

When I was able, I would go on walks re-listening to the
many playlists and songs sent to me but there was a piece
of audio I downloaded to walk around town to the story
of The Chinese Farmer by Alan Watts.

The story goes something like this:

There is a farmer with horses. One night the horses break free. His neighbors overhear about the news of his missing horses so they come by to give their support.
"Oh I'm so sorry about your horses. This is awful…"
Says one neighbour.
The farmer replies, "Maybe."
The neighbors a little surprised by his nonchalant reply think,
"Well that's good, he's handling it well."
The next day, his horses return with 4 beautiful wild horses. The neighbors hear of this news, they come by to congratulate him.

"That's amazing, this is great news!" says a neighbour.
The farmer's reply, "Maybe."
The neighbors at this point are thinking, "What the heck …ok. He should be grateful."

The next day, the farmer's son is training one of the wild horses. The son falls off the horse and breaks his leg.
The neighbors rush by,
"Oh no! I'm so sorry about your son. I heard he broke his leg, that's awful."

Surprise, surprise the farmer's reply is, "Maybe."

The next day the military comes by ready to enlist all the sons in the town. The farmer's son is not picked due to his injury. The neighbors come by to say,

"What a relief! Your son doesn't have to go to war. That's great news!"

The farmer's reply,

"Maybe."

> "It's really impossible to tell whether anything that happens in [life] is good or bad — because you never know what will be the consequence of the misfortune; or you never know what will be the consequences of good fortune."
> — Alan Watts.

So I would walk around, breathe in the fresh spring air, never giving a definitive answer about this whole cancer experience. I'd finish my walk with a deep breath. Lift my head to the sun for some warmth, only for a moment because whichever of the many drugs I was on didn't allow you to be in the sun. Although, I'd think 'maybe' this isn't so bad? 'Maybe' this will be a good thing? **Maybe.**

God only knows... There is nothing new under the sun.
I am reminded of a fellow lymphomie friend that said,

> "It is scary to get diagnosed with this but at the same time, you should always know that you're not going to be the first one ever to go through this. It might seem like you're all alone and no one is able to understand you but in fact there's a whole community out there."
> — Eeva from *Spotlight by Sgoodz* on YouTube.

I reiterate this to myself,
I am not the first.
Sadly, I won't be the last but what I have is this moment and what I can do in this moment.

DING DING
RING BELL

And just like that…it was over. I was done chemo. If that felt blunt to read and very anti-climactic that is exactly how it felt. I went in to my Oncologists office after finishing a PET scan. Seemed like any other day. The routine of a regular blood work, and scans results.

We were waiting on the results to see how much more chemo I'd need. My Mom and Dad were with me waiting. I was sitting on the examination table with my legs dangling over the side which made me feel even more like a child while having to rely on my parents to drive me everywhere, make me food, while sleeping in my pink childhood bedroom.

My oncologist came in and told me I was done. I was in remission and didn't have to do anymore chemo.

As I was still processing this, tears just began to fall before I even realized I was crying. He was quick to give me a tissue box and the next thing I knew he and the nurse were ready to take out my PICC line.
"Deep breath out"
"No Sarah! Deep breath out!"
I was trying not to hyperventilate I took a huge breath IN as they pulled it out. The feeling was jarring and unsettling.

Just like that. That's it. It was over?
I asked my oncologist if I could ring the bell.

There is a gold bell in the hospital that marks the completion of cancer treatment. You ring the bell when you're done treatment.

He was surprised that I wanted to, he said,
"Isn't that kind of cheesy?"

Cheesy or not.
I was in shock and I needed to contextualize that this was truly over.
I needed to ring that bell, and ring it loud for closure.
When he realized that it meant something to me, he corrected himself by saying,
"Ring it so loud that I can hear it."
We were on the third floor. The bell was located on the 4th floor which was the chemo floor. I only heard one person during my whole stay there ring it. So I was determined to make sure people would remember how loud it rang that day. I wanted them to crave that moment like I did when I heard it. I am a force and I will be heard. When we got up there many of the cancer patients were nodding off in their chemo chairs.
I took my camera out, hit record, gave it to my parents. I rang that bell SO LOUD.
DING DING, DING! DONE

THIS IS MY FIGHT SONG PROVE THEM ALL WRONG

Once upon a time
They called me Baldie Locks bish
Cancer tried to get me
but it'd have to
Make A Wish
Had that tumor humour baby
Bad blooded but never beat
"Sugar causes cancer"
It's a good thing I ain't sweet.

SURVIVOR'S GUILT:

75

to put it simply
it's the feeling of guilt that you survived cancer while others did not.
You blame yourself or feel embarrassed or ashamed of lifestyle choices and habits before or after cancer.
It's the emotional weight of feeling guilty, confused or resentful and unsure of how to live "a purposeful life" afterwards.
Constantly thinking,
"Why was I lucky and others weren't?"
"Am I doing enough?"
"Is this how I should be living?"
Feeling immense pressure to live a life with gratitude, happiness or success, all the time. Most likely, the reason I'm even writing this book in the first place.

It's funny but a lot of times your support dies when you actually make it into remission

I think people see the journey of cancer like a marathon. The cancer patient is running this marathon; you have a support team rallying around you, cheering you on.

You can do it!

You're told there is a finish line once you're done treatment.

You cross that finish line only to realize it wasn't the end but just a lap around the track.

Tired and beaten up, you continue on but this time there is no team, no support, no one cares, few are relatable. They're tired of keeping up with you.

Your path isn't paved;
there is no clear direction after cancer. I
It's not a pretty path paved, it's a messy one through the mud and jungle.
It's a path you have to carve out yourself.
You search for answers but only find zero results on how to live life after cancer.

This Place is a Ghost Town

Did I get ghosted or did I ghost them?
It's all been such a blur of uncertainty and emotional turmoil.
Yet I keep checking to see if someone messaged me
or to see if I have a new notification.
Little red notifications we salivate
like Ivan Pavlov's dog dinging a bell for treats.

This isn't even social anymore…

THE ECHO HOTEL

Well…I did it again.
It's 12:30am. This place is quiet. Emitting the sound of sleep.
The ambiance of a sleepy town is calming yet lonely.

So I take a late night trip to The Echo Hotel located on memory lane

AKA my gallery of old photos displayed on my laptop screen.

Glowing at night
Photos of us

3:00 am staring at the ceiling,
Missing you or the memories of simpler times?

I miss it all.

But I'm angry that I do because I never want to be that person who "peaked" or relives the "glory years" when things were better.
When things seemed easy.
I want each year to bring some new wonder into my life.
Enrich me but all I can do in this moment is cry and so I sob.

I'm a tourist in my own world.

This new life is hard but it's given me so much depth, maturity, and wisdom that I can't wish it away. I want this new life to be great but the pressure society puts on cancer survivors is immense. Another reason I've turned to God instead.

God has a plan and sometimes you need to sit in a pit to understand he will get you out of it. I believe in his healing. It's divine timing versus the present impatience I put on myself by not always seeing the bigger picture.

I miss my old self. I look at old photos from the "before" I'm reunited once more.

Oh this gallery of fractured identities.

I'm a tourist in my own life.

I am my own familiar stranger.

It's been 5 years since I visited myself.
It's strange to look at my reflection in a mirror
or see myself with long hair that will only get longer.
Slowly, I begin to look like the person I remember before cancer.
I look only to see inner reflection.
I stare back only to notice slight changes.

I look like how I remember only a little older and also just different.
I am an echo of myself, kind of distant but with a lingering feeling of home.
It's like missing years of your life and teleporting back to

your old self but being a new person, almost a stranger in an old body with some scars to remember that it wasn't all a dream. There are often many "before " and "after" bodies but very few somebodies.
I want to be somebody. I need to be.

At times, grief stricken or filled with the warmth of what was.
I take these reflection trips every few months adding more to my collection for this gallery of my own.

Teleport my eyes back in time and take my heart to places of the past.
I'm taking mental trips.
My life now fractured into before, during and after segments from sickness.

I'm sitting with the bright glow of my laptop while tears are streaming down my face. Calmly, melancholy calls and photos echo,

"The familiar stranger is you."

I click out of my private gallery of images marked by time.
I try not to spend too much time on the cloud because you can get lost up there.
I need to ground myself, come down from the "what if's" and plant my feet on solid ground.

"Till next time."

The echo hotel, it's not a home just a place to check in and check out the past.

I unplug for now, disconnect from the memories and close my laptop

I'm sure I'll be back with more pictures to add for the bigger picture and for the pixelated mosaic of my life.

I leave for now and for now I am.

"Till next time."

I echo back to The Echo Hotel.

ONLINE DATING

I went on a date with a guy.
My hair was short at the time.
A pixie-length style not by choice
but I tried to rock it.
I matched him on a dating app.

The date went well, we texted for a while.
He asked me, "Are you going to keep your hair short?"
He told me he prefers girls with long hair, particularly red
heads.
Knowing full well I'm a cancer survivor, also not a ginger.
He asked, "How long do you think it'd take to grow your
hair?"
How long…however long it takes for you to understand
how insensitive that is to ask.

I cried in private. Well sobbed but
I told him I understand preferences are great
but to randomly tell me that
It's not like this was a bad haircut.
I watched my hair fall out in clumps.

As if my whole existence
is to please a man that desires long hair.
To say the least, it was over.
He said I'm making a mistake.

I do not wish him great pain but

I do wish him the agony of the mundane.
Where nothing bad happens just…
Forever living in Monday mornings
with an eyelash in his eye
that he can't seem to wipe away
that forever lingers in the back of his eyeball.

I send my regards
for he is unmemorable in work settings.
Beige is his favourite colour.
He considers salt spicy.

The only pain he knows is dry contacts, paper cuts, and
stubbed toes.
Losing his car keys, cell phone, and not being able to find
where the scotch tape begins.
Eating microwavable dinners
where the plate is too hot and the food is simultaneously
still frozen.
Eating dry turkey with nothing to wash it down.

Boring sex. Bad reruns with nothing on TV.
Beach days that are too windy and cloudy.
Wet socks and sand everywhere.

He waves back to people only to realize
they aren't waving at him
but to their friend behind him.
Oh the agony!

He is the embodiment of bleakness and dread.
He is that feeling of Friday being too far away.

But most of all,

these tiny yet insufferable moments
are all he'll ever know so he *can't* complain.
His life is sad but no one is sad for him.

Maybe I should take a break from dating apps.

I HAVE A STALKER

I caught him once but it doesn't feel like he's gone.
I still feel his lingering presence.

Last time, he got the best of me.
He consumed me. My body. My thoughts.
Everything was about him.
He even changed the way my friends and family viewed
me.

Now I'm scared he's back.
Maybe he's not with me?
But tampering with things? My water? The food I eat?
Is he with the people I love?

Where is he?

Is he ever truly gone?

I heard he was with my Aunt once
but I was too young to understand
so it became unspoken knowledge.
Even a neighbour.

It happened to a friend of a friend of mine.
Now my mom's best friend.

You just hope you catch him early
So he doesn't get the best of you.

When I go out I sometimes think I see him
in the corner of my eye.
Sometimes with strangers?
Possibly taunting them
and you think maybe he forgot about me?
But every night you picture looking out your window
and seeing a shadowy figure near a dim lamp-post
but he's not that cliché.

Sometimes it feels like he's
right around the corner...
or even in the room?
This looming presence
is suffocating but you can't think like that.
You have to stay positive and not disappoint those around
you

So you eventually drift off to sleep
after endless worries mixed into the covers
with every shift and turn.
Don't think about it.

Move on.
I finally adjust to a comfortable position
and wake up wondering how much sleep I actually got.
I try to start a new day
though I can't help but wonder...was he here
and possibly still?

Cancer is my stalker.
My obsession
My worry but how can I not think of him?

He's on the news.

They write movies about him
He's in everything.
Possibly tampering with my food and water
or worse with the people I love.

You either die from him
or you get enough of a breath to escape him
only to see him everywhere else but with you.

So how can I not think of him?
He's a stalker.
I caught him once
but it never truly feels like he's gone.

It's almost a bad relationship that I can't ever get out of.
You just hope you catch him early enough
so you can live only to see him everywhere

Everywhere else but with you.

THE END?

Dear Shakespeare,
We all deserve a happy ending
Pending…pending…pending…
Pending…pending…

My heart screaming: Don't die!
This isn't your ending…
This isn't your ending!
The thing about cancer is
it never truly answers

life's big questions.

I survived
Now I have to learn
How to live
The rest of my life

The curious wait
for a resolution.
The End or Fin-ish?

They want to hear a happy ending.
She got a meaningful tattoo.
She went on an adventure to find
the Eat Pray Love life.
She met a man and got married.
She ran the marathon and won first place.

Oh the life after cancer,
If they don't kill you off as the sick character
The movie ends once treatment ends
The credits roll
Congratulations you didn't die
Now good luck
with the rest of your life
To always be happy
To never ever be ungrateful
To know how to live perfectly
after so many years of just surviving
To tell others the secrets of
dancing with death
and living to tell tales
Provide secret wisdom
from an illness that takes so much.
Only to sometimes drunkenly utter words while wobbling
trying to meet those curious eyes looking for insight
at night under city lights
only to tell them,

"Hey, sometimes you just don't die."
And stumble away.

No cowboy riding into the sunset
or a freeze frame moment.
No awesome music playing with a whole production team
as credits roll.
No standing ovation
No romantic vacation
No, it's a silent walk away from the Doctor's room.
It's less appointments
but still many new waiting rooms.

Because it's never over
I can't give you
The End
to a life I'm still living.
Everyone wants a happy ending but
I just want a happy new start.

So here's to a new chapter unwritten.
To knowing each day on this earth,
I've been surviving, trying, and growing.
Now, I'm finally living.
I am forever grateful that for some crazy reason, I'm still here.
I'm not going to pretend that it hasn't been hard.
There are still moments I feel very burnt out …but I'm learning how to live with uncertainty and how to build a cool life within it.

I'm not writing
The end
I'm writing
To scream "I MADE IT."
To learn new life lessons.
To unlearn old ways
To understanding, I am not healed but I am healing.
To carry on and accept I am not cured but I am healthy.
To truly knowing not everything is guaranteed but I am ok with it.
And finally, I hope the same for you.
Here's to us and a new start because

This isn't 'The End' it's The Start.

THE WATER THAT CLEANS YOU

After every hospital visit, I showered.
During my chemo-sessions, I only drank water.
Water is therapy.

We are like plants
We water ourselves
showering
our mind with ideas
on how to grow
You cannot plant a seed
and expect the end goal

It's a process
like water
just flow
let it come
let it go

We are like plants
Watering ourselves
showering
our mind with ideas
on how to grow
Ponder lightly.
Don't drown yourself
in thought.
Some thoughts will go down the drain

Let the ideas trickle down
like the water that cleans you.

You can't control which drop falls where

Darling these aren't tears
It's just the way
the water falls

THE SILENT AWARENESS.

Faint ripples
rise and fall
come and go

the ocean of being
bodies of water
the waves
never stop coming
but we flow
rise and fall
come and go

The quiet restart
The second birth
The silent awareness

Looking at life as it is…as it just is

At this very moment,

The world is blossoming into
infinite variety of divine creation
then falling silent in amazement
at its own miracle

faint ripples
rise and fall
come and go

the silent awareness of the universe realizing itself.

It is a loud yet silent realization

You are here.

"SECOND BIRTH"

When awareness has become fully aware of itself.

At a certain point,
life has no more secrets to uncover, to learn, or to reveal.

The duality of life and death is gone, replaced by an unshakable contentment.

We reach this stage of freedom, life starts over, which is why 'enlightenment' is often referred to as 'second birth.'

Today, enlightenment is no longer the goal of life.

The most a teacher can do is to reopen the door again (possibly a revolving one?).

I asked myself the 3 age-old questions:

1. Who Am I?
2. Where did I come from?
3. Why am I here?

1. You are the whole universe
2. You came from a source that was never born
3. You are here to create the world in every moment, every passage of time, to experience itself.

Once you gain this knowledge, it's like being (re)born or

sometimes (re)minded.
You become timeless, you (re)live outside of time.

God is the source, creator of the story. The author of us.

You will continue to have thoughts, questions and feelings
but now they are soft impulses;
Coming and going
Rising and falling
Faint ripples
Softly entering The Silent Awareness.

ALL THE THINGS YOU NEED TO HEAR:

You are loved.

God connected us.

You are exactly where you need to be, now rest.

God's hands hold you and never let go.

Everything always works out.

The smallest kindnesses that each of us can do go a long way

Like a simple cup of cold water for a thirsty soul

A listening ear in a distracted world

Small gestures show an encouraging world to continue

Comparison is not needed focus on finding your higher self

Shine your light.

THIS IS IT.

ACKNOWLEDGMENTS:

99

Thank you to my family, friends, and those with faith.

Thank you to my editor Andy Milanarsky.

ABOUT THE AUTHOR:

Sarah Josephine Gooderham was born April 25th 1994.
She lives in The Greater Toronto Area of
Ontario, Canada.
She was diagnosed with Hodgkin's Lymphoma stage 2B
at the age of 22 years old. This is her first poetry book
published. She travels frequently and enjoys a good
bowl of soup.

@sgoodzgirl
Sarah.gooderham@icloud.com
www.youtube.com/sgoodz